THE SCIENCE OF **SPEED**

# THE SCIENCE OF BICYCLE RACING

### BY SUZANNE SLADE

CONSULTANT:
PAUL OHMANN, PH.D
ASSOCIATE PROFESSOR AND CHAIR OF PHYSICS
UNIVERSITY OF ST. THOMAS, MINNESOTA

CAPSTONE PRESS
a capstone imprint

Velocity is published by Capstone Press,
1710 Roe Crest Drive, North Mankato, Minnesota 56003.
www.capstonepub.com

**Library of Congress Cataloging-in-Publication Data**
Slade, Suzanne, author.
  The science of bicycle racing / by Suzanne Slade.
    pages cm.—(Velocity--the science of speed)
  Audience: Ages 10–14.
  Audience: Grades 4 to 6.
  Summary: "Describes the science concepts involved in several types of bicycle racing"—
Provided by publisher.
  ISBN 978-1-4765-3909-6 (library binding)
  ISBN 978-1-4765-5192-0 (pbk.)
  ISBN 978-1-4765-6057-1 (ebook PDF)
  1. Bicycle racing—Juvenile literature. 2. Cycling—Juvenile literature. I. Title. II. Series:
Velocity (Capstone Press)
  GV1049.S53 2014
  796.6'2—dc23                                                                    2013027046

**Editorial Credits**
Adrian Vigliano, editor; Kyle Grenz, designer; Laura Manthe, production specialist

**Photo Credits**
Alamy: Seb Rogers, 39 (top); Dreamstime: Lukas Blazek, 43, Mark Eaton, 28, 30 (left), Valeria
Cantone, 30 (right), Yuriy Chaban, 37 (right); Getty Images: Aurora+/Jeff Zimmerman, 42,
Christian Pondella, 19, Jonathan Daniel, 15; Newscom: Actionplus/Dan Jocelyn, 17, EPA,
14, Getty Images/AFP/Franck Fife, 26, Getty Images/AFP/Leon Neal, 4, Image Broker/
NielsDK, 16, RTR/RNGS, 27 (map), ZUMA Press/Mike Albright, 41 (top), ZUMA Press/
Steven Paston, 29 (top); Shutterstock: Albert Fedchenko, 27 (croissant), Angyalosi Beata,
12, Anke van Wyk, 21 (inset), avarand, 22, 22-23, Bart_J, 27 (pasta), bergamont, 13, Dmitry
Naumov, 36 (both), Dmitry Yashkin, 31, Doug James, cover, Dziewul, 25 (both), FCG,
39 (bottom), 40, filip robert, 6, 7, 9, fotographic1980, (background, throughout), Gena73,
10, gielmichal, 37 (left), gkordus, 20, homydesign, 8, 45, Jan de Wild, 38, Jean-Francois
Rivard, 35 (bottom), 44 (bottom), Layland Masuda, 27 (drink), maga, 34, Maxim Petrichuk,
32, Mirvav, 41 (bottom), Picsfive, 27 (energy bar), Radu Razvan, 21, Rena Schild, 23, 24,
Sergiy Zavgorodny, 35 (top), Stefan Schurr, 44 (top), Tim UR, 27 (chicken), vetroff, 37 (top);
Wikimedia: mistagregory, 29 (bottom)

Printed in the United States of America in Stevens Point, Wisconsin.
092013      007767WZS14

# TABLE OF CONTENTS

# Olympic Speed

The biggest race of Maris Strombergs' life was about to start—the 2012 Olympic BMX Men's Finals. The buzzer sounded. Strombergs pedaled furiously down the steep ramp. He raced up the first hill, leaped into the air, and landed on the backside of the next hill. Then he gained speed and flew over the next pair of hills. Spying a tight turn ahead, he leaned low, knowing sharp curves wipe out unprepared riders. Strombergs soared over dozens more hills until he saw the finish line ahead. Legs throbbing, he kept pushing and raced across the line—first! He had won the gold medal!

The bike and rider are traveling at a certain **velocity**.

## BMX Beginnings

BMX stands for bicycle motocross. BMX became popular after the movie *On Any Sunday* was released in 1971. The movie showed people in California riding bikes modified to look like motorcycles. The people in the movie rode over dirt hills and flat valleys. Soon bikes specially made for BMX were available, and kids across the country gave them a try.

**Traction** gives the rider grip between the bike tire and the road.

**velocity**—the speed an object travels in a certain direction
**traction**—the amount of grip between two surfaces in contact with each other

4

New technologies and equipment continue to make cycling sports faster and better than ever. Cyclists work hard to improve their speed through training, but science also gives racers an extra edge.

**Maris Strombergs**

**Air resistance** pushes against the bike and rider.

**Gravity** pulls down on rider and bike.

**air resistance**—the force the air puts on an object moving through it

**gravity**—a force that pulls objects toward the center of Earth

# Chapter 1

# Science of Bicycling Basics

## MUSCLE TO MOTION

Behind the starting gate, BMX riders stand on their pedals as they wait for the race to begin. Leg muscles bursting with energy, the seconds tick by slowly. When the gate finally lowers, racers release their muscle energy and pedal around the track at top speeds.

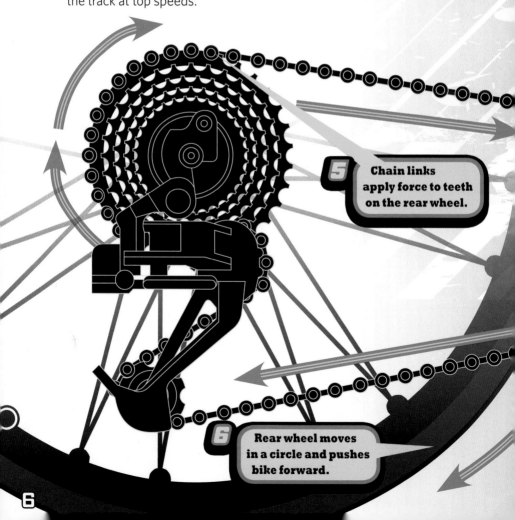

**5** Chain links apply force to teeth on the rear wheel.

**6** Rear wheel moves in a circle and pushes bike forward.

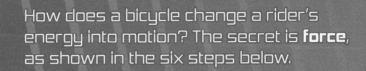

How does a bicycle change a rider's energy into motion? The secret is **force**, as shown in the six steps below.

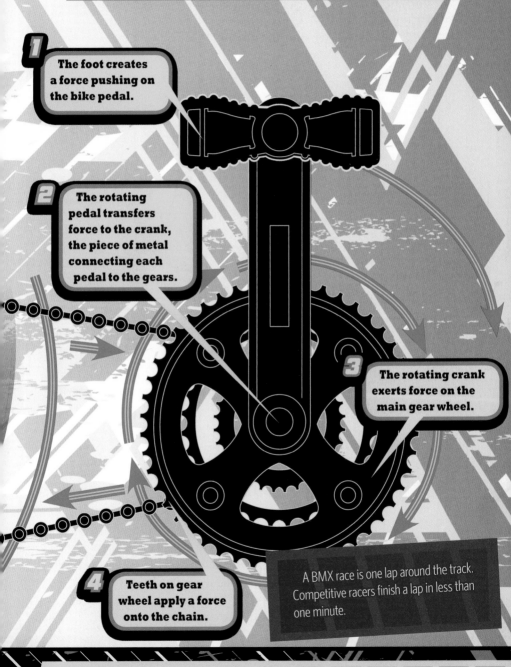

**1** The foot creates a force pushing on the bike pedal.

**2** The rotating pedal transfers force to the crank, the piece of metal connecting each pedal to the gears.

**3** The rotating crank exerts force on the main gear wheel.

**4** Teeth on gear wheel apply a force onto the chain.

A BMX race is one lap around the track. Competitive racers finish a lap in less than one minute.

**force**—a factor (such as pushing or pulling) that causes something to change its speed

# PUTTIN' ON THE BRAKES

As a rider and a bike speed over a race course they both have **momentum**. The momentum of a moving object equals its **mass** times its velocity. Mass is the amount of matter in a rider, bike, and equipment. The more the mass and the faster the speed, the greater the racer's momentum.

Momentum =
mass x velocity

Braking skills are essential for racers. Proper braking controls momentum and slows down riders to prevent them from hitting other riders. Braking also keeps racers from wiping out on tight turns. Braking on turns helps riders maintain the traction they need to keep bikes balanced.

**momentum**—the force or speed created by movement
**mass**—the amount of matter in something; matter is anything that has weight and takes up space

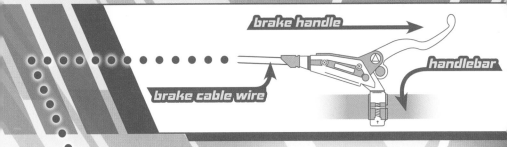

brake handle

handlebar

brake cable wire

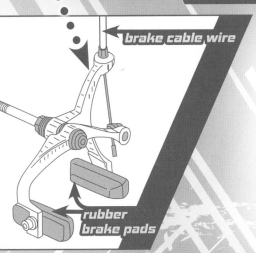

brake cable wire

rubber brake pads

Most bikes have rim brakes, which are activated when the rider squeezes the brake handle. Squeezing the brake handle puts **tension** on the brake cable wire. Under tension, the cable pulls the two brake levers with rubber brake pads around the tire, pinching the wheel rim.

As a rider slows down, the forward momentum is changed into heat. **Friction** between the brake pads and metal wheel rim causes the pads and rim to both heat up slightly.

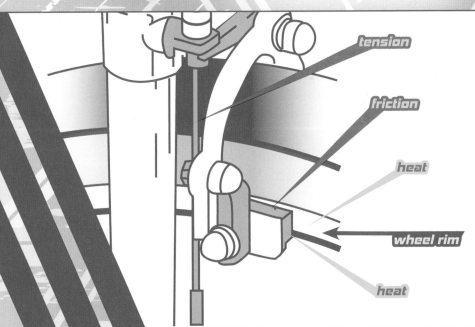

tension

friction

heat

wheel rim

heat

**tension**—the stress, such as tightness or stiffness, that results from stretching or pulling

**friction**—the resistance caused by one surface moving over another

# THE BICYCLE MACHINE

How does a vehicle with a frame, two wheels, and pedals climb hills, fly over jumps, and make tight turns? Perhaps a bicycle is not as simple as you think.

A simple machine does work with only one movement. There are six kinds of simple machines: lever, pulley, inclined plane, wheel and axle, wedge, and screw. A bicycle is made of three simple machines, so it is actually a complex machine.

pulley

axle

fulcrum

wheel

lever

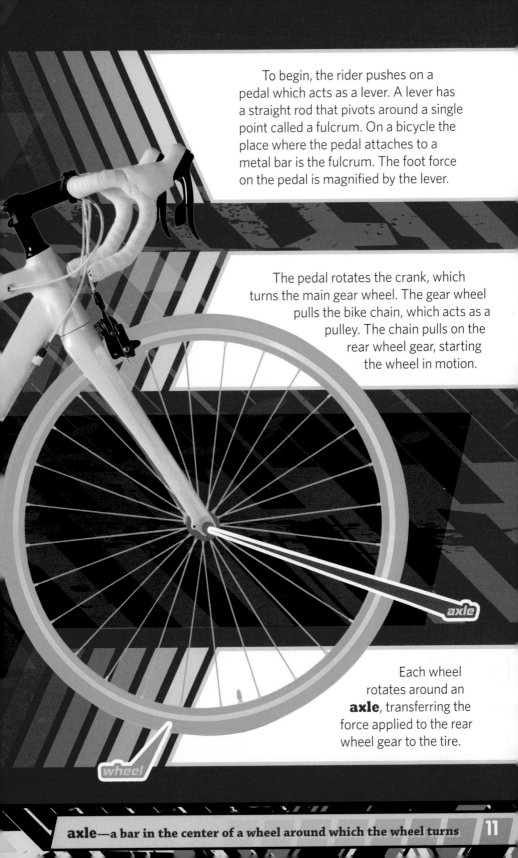

To begin, the rider pushes on a pedal which acts as a lever. A lever has a straight rod that pivots around a single point called a fulcrum. On a bicycle the place where the pedal attaches to a metal bar is the fulcrum. The foot force on the pedal is magnified by the lever.

The pedal rotates the crank, which turns the main gear wheel. The gear wheel pulls the bike chain, which acts as a pulley. The chain pulls on the rear wheel gear, starting the wheel in motion.

axle

Each wheel rotates around an **axle**, transferring the force applied to the rear wheel gear to the tire.

wheel

**axle**—a bar in the center of a wheel around which the wheel turns

# WEIGHT AND BALANCE

A bike is designed so it distributes weight evenly to keep the rider balanced. Proper weight distribution keeps a rider from falling backward when pedaling up a hill or flying over the handlebars when coasting down a hill. This balancing act starts with a bike's triangular frame. The frame's angled bars move some of a rider's weight on the seat to the front tire.

triangular frame

A bike rider sits over the rear wheel, but both wheels must support an equal share of the rider's weight. To do this a bike frame distributes a rider's weight evenly to both wheels.

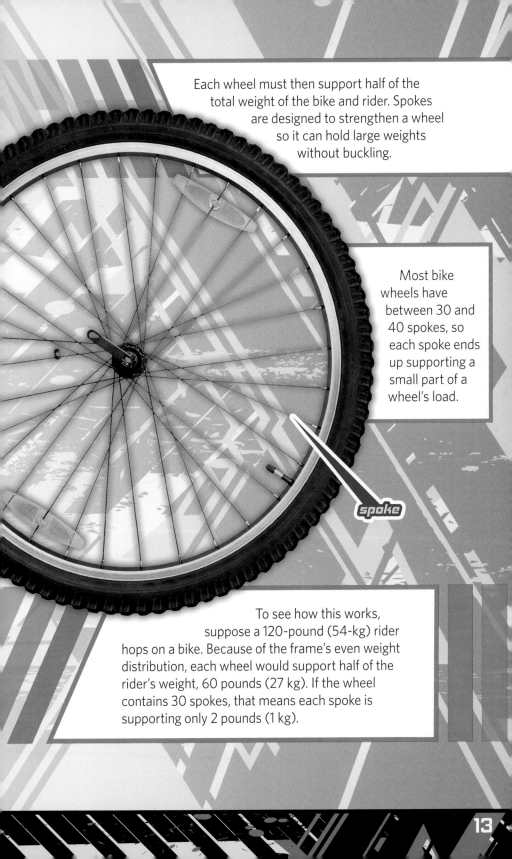

Each wheel must then support half of the total weight of the bike and rider. Spokes are designed to strengthen a wheel so it can hold large weights without buckling.

Most bike wheels have between 30 and 40 spokes, so each spoke ends up supporting a small part of a wheel's load.

spoke

To see how this works, suppose a 120-pound (54-kg) rider hops on a bike. Because of the frame's even weight distribution, each wheel would support half of the rider's weight, 60 pounds (27 kg). If the wheel contains 30 spokes, that means each spoke is supporting only 2 pounds (1 kg).

# CRASH, BASH!

Even the most experienced riders end up in crashes. Crashes can be caused by several factors. Some racers simply lose their balance during the heat of a race, while others bump into another rider's tire.

Track racers use ultra thin tires with reduced weight for better speed. But these narrow tires provide less surface area, or contact on the track. Less surface area causes the tires to have reduced grip or traction. With less traction it's easier for riders to slip.

Heat while skidding on track

bent frame

**FACT**

Kinetic energy equals one-half the rider's mass times the rider's speed squared.

$$\tfrac{1}{2}MV^2$$

Crashes also happen when racers don't apply brakes evenly. Too much braking on front wheel brakes can cause the front tire to stop quickly. The rider's momentum then can cause him or her to continue moving forward—right over the handlebars.

Momentum throws this rider over the handlebars.

As a rider speeds around a track, motion gives the rider **kinetic energy**. When a biker falls, that energy doesn't disappear. At impact, a rider's kinetic energy disperses. The resulting forces may snap frames, fracture bones, dent helmets, or bend handlebars and wheels. For riders falling on a smooth track surface, kinetic energy may also become heat on both of the skidding surfaces.

# Chapter 2

# BMX Racing

## TACKLING THE HILLS

After hours of training, BMX racers know the best way to attack the hills on a track. When it comes to **doubles**, jumping from the top of one hill to the other is the fastest option. To make this leap, racers speed up an angled hill to overcome the force of gravity and take flight. When landing, riders keep their legs extended. Their legs act like shock absorbers to reduce the impact force when their tires hit the ground.

A rhythm section is a bunch of small hills close together. Keeping wheels on the ground is the fastest way to attack a rhythm section. Making many small jumps would create too much air resistance pushing against a rider, causing a loss in speed.

air resistance

gravity

impact force

**double**—two steep hills close together on a BMX race course

**FACT**

To reduce the effects of air resistance during a race, riders stay crouched low over their seats with their knees pointing forward. This position helps the air flow more smoothly across the rider.

On smaller hills that are farther apart, some racers keep pedaling on the way up and down. Others prefer pumping. To pump, a rider coasts up the front side of a hill. On the backside, he or she pushes down on the handlebars while standing on both pedals and pushing with his or her feet. Pumping lets the arms and legs act like shock absorbers. This technique allows the bike to move over hills smoothly and gain momentum.

# CASE STUDY: FREESTYLE

Freestyle BMX riders are all about stunts, not speed. But science helps riders perform better stunts too!

## FIVE TYPES OF FREESTYLE

| | |
|---|---|
| Flatland | Riders do tricks on flat surfaces such as parking lots and basketball courts. |
| Street | Riders do tricks on common obstacles found in streets. |
| Park | Riders perform tricks in skateparks with wood, concrete, and metal structures. |
| Trails | Riders do jumps off of piles of well-packed dirt. |
| Vert | Riders speed up half-pipes and fly into the air to do tricks. |

## BREAKING DOWN THE 360 TRICK

A 360 is a vert trick where a rider spins the bike in a complete circle in the air. To start, the rider zooms down one side of the half-pipe and shoots up the other. Right before the bike leaves the half-pipe, the rider turns his head and handlebars sharply in the same direction. After rotating 360 degrees, the rider straightens the handlebars before landing safely on the ramp.

**half-pipe**—U-shaped ramp bikers use to perform jumps and other maneuvers

Let's examine the scientific forces at work in this spectacular move:

A bike slows down as it reaches the highest point of a jump. This gives the rider more time to spin around, making it seem as if both bike and rider are floating.

At the highest point of the jump, the rider's speed is zero.

Earth's gravity causes all free-falling objects to accelerate toward earth at a constant rate of 32.2 feet per second squared (9.8 m/s2). For every second an object is falling, its speed increases 32.2 feet per second.

**FACT**

Some professional BMX vert riders compete on a mega ramp in the X Games' Big Air event. The mega ramp is a whopping 62 feet (19 meters) high and 293 feet (89 meters) long.

# Chapter 3:

# Hitting the Road

## WEIGHT MATTERS

Road cyclists spend hours each week riding hundreds of miles on smooth, asphalt roads during training.

Bike weight is important in road racing because it takes more energy to push a heavier weight. By using less energy, riders can increase their speeds. Riders carefully consider the weight of each bike component. Fractions of an ounce make a big difference in the energy a rider uses on long rides.

Pro racers ride bikes weighing around 14 pounds (6 kg). An average non-racing bike weighs closer to 30 pounds (13 kg). Pro bike frame materials such as titanium and lightweight carbon fiber help reduce weight.

Riders even choose the lightest weight water bottles. In addition to minimizing bike weight, road cyclists try to maintain a low, but healthy, body weight.

Wheel weight is also crucial. Riders push wheel weight in circles for the entire ride. Many racers use heavy, durable wheels for training rides. Then they switch to lightweight carbon fiber wheels for races. Wheels with thin discs in the center instead of metal spokes also cut weight.

① **saddle**
thin, narrow seat

② **frame**
high-end carbon fiber racing frame

③ **water bottle**
lightweight bottle; a rider takes only as much water as he or she will need during a race

④ **fork**
made of carbon fiber

⑤ **crankset**
made of carbon fiber

⑥ **tires**
weight depends on tire thickness and width

⑦ **gears**
made of carbon fiber

⑧ **wheels**
carbon fiber wheels for races; heavier wheels for training

# AERODYNAMICS

Air resistance works against road-racing cyclists. To cut down on air resistance and ride their fastest, cyclists wear tight shorts and fitted jerseys. Some top riders even have their jerseys specially tailored so they fit like a second skin.

A smooth **aerodynamic** helmet also cuts down on air resistance. Some road-racing bikes have two sets of handlebars. The inner set of handlebars reduces air resistance by allowing the rider's elbows to be tucked in close together. Cyclists lean over their bikes to create the least amount of air resistance on their bodies. Many competitive riders shave their legs and arms, leaving them with smooth skin to reduce air resistance even more.

**aerodynamic—built to move easily through the air**

Bikes are designed to reduce air resistance too. Frame designs with flattened, thinner aerodynamic tubes have less air resistance than circular tubes. A solid cover placed over rear wheels reduces air resistance on bike spokes.

**FACT**
Up to 90% of a racer's work goes to overcome air resistance.

# RIDING THE DRAFT

A stage race is a long road race that lasts several days or weeks. Each day cyclists ride one stage, or part, of the race. Stage races include a variety of stages such as "flats" where the road is relatively flat. During other "mountainous" days riders make grueling climbs before screaming down steep descents. Some stage races start with a short, fast time trial.

Many stage races involve teams, not just individual riders. In team stage racing, every rider has a job. Teams have designated top riders whose goal is to win the race.

Other riders support them. Riders known as domestiques take turns riding in front of top riders to "pull" them by creating a **slipstream**.

Riding in the slipstream is called drafting. Riders experience less air resistance while drafting. A rider's front tire must be very close to the domestique's back tire to ride in the slipstream. The faster riders travel, the more benefit they get from drafting.

Cyclists from many teams often ride together in a pack called a peloton so they can draft off each other and conserve energy. Peloton riders are closely packed together, so they must be careful their tires don't bump others and cause a crash.

**slipstream**—a path of moving air behind a moving object    **25**

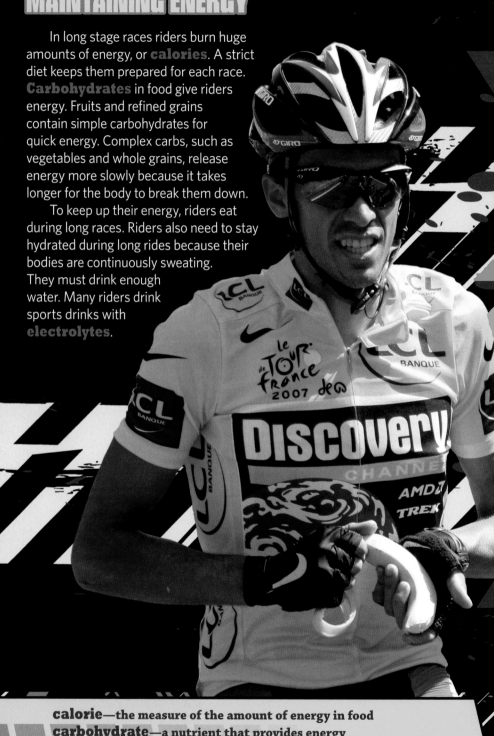

In long stage races riders burn huge amounts of energy, or **calories**. A strict diet keeps them prepared for each race. **Carbohydrates** in food give riders energy. Fruits and refined grains contain simple carbohydrates for quick energy. Complex carbs, such as vegetables and whole grains, release energy more slowly because it takes longer for the body to break them down.

To keep up their energy, riders eat during long races. Riders also need to stay hydrated during long rides because their bodies are continuously sweating. They must drink enough water. Many riders drink sports drinks with **electrolytes**.

**calorie**—the measure of the amount of energy in food
**carbohydrate**—a nutrient that provides energy
**electrolyte**—a mineral which helps produce and store energy and regulate fluid in the body

# The Tour de France

The Tour de France is an annual stage race in France where riders cycle about 2,000 miles (3,200 km) in 21 days. During a single stage, cyclists burn an average of 4,000 to 5,000 calories. That number jumps to 8,000 calories during mountain climbing stages.

## The 100th Tour de France
The 2013 tour of France road cycling race takes place from June 29 to July 21.

| START | | | | | | | | | Rest day | | | | | Rest day | | | | FINISH |
|---|---|---|---|---|---|---|---|---|---|---|---|---|---|---|---|---|---|---|---|
| Stage | 1 | 2 | 3 | 4 | 5 | 6 | 7 | 8 | 9 | 10 | 11 | 12 | 13 | 14 | 15 | 16 | 17 | 18 | 19 | 20 | 21 |
| Km | 213 | 156 | 146 | 25 | 229 | 277 | 206 | 195 | 169 | 197 | 33 | 218 | 173 | 191 | 243 | 168 | 32 | 173 | 205 | 125 | 134 |
| Jun. | 29 | 30 | Jul. 1 | 2 | 3 | 4 | 5 | 6 | 7 | 9 | 10 | 11 | 12 | 13 | 14 | 16 | 17 | 18 | 19 | 20 | 21 |

Total: 3,404 km*

- ○—○ Stage
- ○—○ Time-trial stage
- ○—○ Mountain stage
- ····· Transfer

Source: Amaury Sport Organisation    *Stages may not add up exactly due to rounding

## A sample Tour de France rider's menu on a mountain climbing day (not including water):

### Breakfast:
one banana
one-third pound pasta
one-third pound cereal
one croissant
half-pound mixed fruit
10 ounces orange juice
8 ounces coffee

### Pre-race meal:
one-third pound pasta

### During the race:
four energy bars
128 ounces energy drink
two meat sandwiches

### After race:
32 ounces recovery drink
one meat sandwich
one energy bar
two sweets

### Dinner:
half-pound pasta
half-pound mixed vegetables
half-pound chicken breast
12 ounces yogurt
5 ounces fruit

# Chapter 4:
# Taking it to the Track

## THE VELODROME

High-speed track racing takes place on a velodrome. This special oval-shaped track has two straight sections with 180-degree turns at each end.

tire friction

Have you ever felt pushed against a door while in a car making a sharp turn? That's **centrifugal force**. When we go around a curve, our body's momentum still wants to go in a straight line. This pushes us to the outside of a turn. It is the same for bicycle racers. The steep angles of the velodrome help reduce this centrifugal force.

**centrifugal force**—an outward push an object experiences as it moves in a circular path

## Fast Velodromes

The London Olympic committee wanted to build an especially fast velodrome for the 2012 games. Designers worked to create a track with high-banking turns. The building was also designed for precise temperature control. High temperatures keep riders' muscles loose. Warm air is also less **dense** than cool air. Air with less density reduces air resistance on riders.

During races riders travel at speeds between 30 and 40 miles (48 and 64 kilometers) per hour. So velodrome tracks are built at an angle to keep riders in. The track angles vary in different velodromes. Most tracks are designed so racers can reach speeds up to 45 miles (72 kilometers) per hour.

## 2012 Olympic velodrome facts:

-35 miles (56 km) of wood and 300,000 nails used

-took two years and $150 million to complete

-temperature carefully controlled at 82.4 degrees Fahrenheit (28 degrees Celsius)

180° turn

# SHAPED FOR SPEED

Racers often wear special tear-drop shaped helmets called aero helmets during time trials and short track races. An aero helmet is curved in front like a regular bike helmet to reduce air resistance.But aero helmets have a unique pointed tail, or extension, in back. The tail provides a smooth line from the back of the head over the neck. This extension prevents **turbulent air flow**.

To be effective, an aero helmet must be positioned so there is very little space between the bottom of the helmet tail and the rider's back. The helmet makes the air flow more smoothly over the helmet and across the rider's back. This smooth air flow helps a rider go faster.

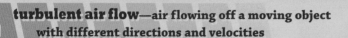

**turbulent air flow**—air flowing off a moving object with different directions and velocities

# Protect Your Head

A helmet is essential in all forms of biking to prevent head injuries. Helmets are made of a lightweight foam interior covered with a plastic outer shell. Sometimes soft cloth pads are attached to the foam to make the helmet more comfortable. But the crushable foam interior is what protects the head. If a rider falls and hits his or her head on the ground, the foam crushes and absorbs some of the impact energy. The crushing spreads the force out over a longer time. This reduces the peak impact, which means fewer head and brain injuries.

graph showing impact energy on a brain during fall for rider without a helmet

graph showing impact energy on a brain during fall for rider wearing a helmet

Studies have shown wearing an aero helmet instead of a regular helmet saves about 30 to 60 seconds for every hour of riding. In fast time trial races that are won by tenths of a second, an aero helmet can mean the difference between first and second place.

# Chapter 5:

# Mastering the Mountains

## A BUMPY RIDE

Mountain bikers tackle a whole lot more than just mountains. While climbing steep trails they race across rocks, branches, tree roots, and other obstacles. But one thing helps smooth out their bumpy ride—shocks.

Some riders use full-suspension bikes with shocks in the rear and front forks. For longer races and faster sprints, racers often choose a hardtail design with shocks only in the front fork.

Bike shocks have two jobs. First, they keep tires in contact with the trail as much as possible for maximum traction. They also absorb bumps to reduce the impact on the rider.

front fork

Some bike shocks are coil sprung, which means they have metal springs that absorb bumps. Others are air sprung, which means that they have chambers of compressed air to smooth out bumps.

## How a Shock Works

When a bike tire hits an obstacle, it creates an upward force on the bike frame to the rider. A shock absorbs some of that force in the spring movement or air chamber, so the rider feels a smaller upward force or bump. Riders can adjust most bike shocks to provide the right balance of traction and bike bounce.

### front shocks

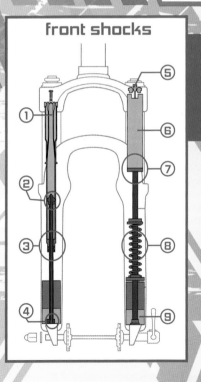

① oil chamber
② rebound piston
③ seal head
④ rebound adjuster
⑤ air valve
⑥ air chamber
⑦ air piston
⑧ negative springs
⑨ lubrication oil

### back shocks

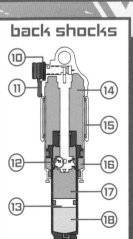

⑩ rebound adjuster
⑪ pro pedal lever
⑫ boost valve
⑬ internal floating piston
⑭ main air chamber
⑮ extra-volume air chamber
⑯ negative air chamber
⑰ oil chamber
⑱ nitrogen chamber

# MOUNTAIN BIKING TIRES AND TREAD

Mountain bikers use wide tires with deep grooves for better traction. Traction is crucial for cyclists who are riding over loose gravel, slick rocks, and wet logs.

Mountain bike tires are usually about 2 inches (5 cm) wide. A wide tire provides better traction because more tire surface area comes in contact with the trail.

When purchasing tires, racers pay close attention to the size of the bumpy knobs in the tread. Smaller knobs have less surface area on the trail. This means less **rolling resistance** for more speed on tightly packed trails. Larger knobs increase surface area contact and rolling resistance. They allow for increased traction in loose sand and mud.

rolling resistance—the force resisting the motion of a body rolling across a surface

Another way bikers get more surface area contact and better traction is by adjusting tire pressure. Mountain bike racers often lower the pressure in their tires.

Lower pressure helps absorb bumps better because the tire has some "give." This softer tire also allows the tire to flatten out slightly more, so more surface area of the tire comes in contact with the trail.

# GET IT IN GEAR

In mountain biking racers use different gears for steep inclines, flat trails, and downhill runs. A multi-gear bike has two derailleurs. Derailleurs move the chain to different sprockets, allowing the rider to shift gears.

A lower gear, or "low gear ratio," causes more pedal rotations per one turn of the bike wheels. A low gear makes it easier to pedal up hills because it requires less foot force. In a bike's lowest gear, the chain is on the smallest sprocket near the pedal and the largest sprocket on the rear wheel.

**low (large) gear**
less foot force;
more pedal rotations

**shifter cable**
adjusts derailleurs

Riders shift to higher gears when heading out on flat terrain. A higher gear slows down how fast the pedals rotate and therefore requires more foot force on the pedals.

**rear derailleur**
moves the chain up and down
sprockets on the rear wheel

High gears provide bike stability while pedaling down hills or at high speeds. This is because the pedals move more slowly for each tire rotation in a high gear. When a bike is in its highest gear, the chain is on the largest sprocket in the front and the smallest sprocket in the rear.

**front derailleur**
moves the chain to different sprockets near the pedal

**gear lever**
is moved up or down to shift to higher and lower gears

**chain**
transfers power from the front sprocket to the rear sprocket

# Chapter 6:

# The Extreme Sport of Cyclo-Cross

## EXPLOSIVE POWER

Cyclo-cross is a type of extreme bike racing that is done in all kinds of weather. A cyclo-cross course is about 1 to 3 miles (1.6 to 4.8 km) long. Riders complete several laps around the course for each race. The course is filled with obstacles and sharp turns.

When approaching the tight turns, racers must slow down to stay inside the course boundaries. These are marked with ribbons strung across wood stakes. To be competitive, riders need explosive leg power to give them quick **acceleration** as they leave each turn.

**acceleration**—the rate of change of speed

# Speeding Downhill

Coasting, or freewheeling, down hills allows bike wheels to spin freely while the rider rests. As the force of gravity wins out against tire friction and air resistance, the bike and rider accelerate.

Cyclo-cross and other kinds of bike racers wear shoes that clip into special bike pedals. These "clipless" pedals allow racers to pull up on pedals as well as push down. With extra force on the pedals, riders are able to gain speed through their entire pedal stroke.

**39**

# KEEP YOUR BALANCE

Cyclo-cross courses include large obstacles racers can't always ride over, such as sand traps, logs, and small streams. Courses also include obstacles like stairs or wood barriers. When meeting these obstacles, riders need to carry their bikes.

The key to a rider maintaining balance while carrying the bike over an obstacle is **center of gravity** (cg). If a rider holds the bike at its center of gravity, then the bike will stay balanced while the rider is running.

**center of gravity—the point at which an object can balance**

Finding the cg of a simple, symmetrical object such as a ball is easy—it's the center of the ball. For a more complex object, such as a bicycle, the cg is not so obvious.

center of gravity

The fastest way to find a bicycle's center of gravity is to hang the top bar of the frame on a hook. Then slide the bike on the hook until you find the point where the bike hangs level. That is the cg where a cyclist would hold the bike during a race.

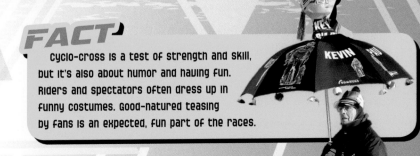

FACT

Cyclo-cross is a test of strength and skill, but it's also about humor and having fun. Riders and spectators often dress up in funny costumes. Good-natured teasing by fans is an expected, fun part of the races.

# UNDER PRESSURE

Cyclo-cross racers try to find a tire pressure which is a good balance of traction and rolling resistance. Tire pressure is affected by a rider's weight because the weight of a racer is a downward force that acts evenly on both tires.

In order to achieve the same traction and rolling resistance, a heavier rider would use a higher tire pressure than a lighter rider would.

# Winter Riding

Cyclo-cross racers keep competing through the winter, which means riding through slippery piles of snow. Riders use a special kind of tire called a tubular tire on snowy days to get more traction. Tubular tires are glued directly onto the wheel rims. They require less air pressure than regular tires. And importantly, these softer, flatter tires provide more traction on snow.

tubular tire

# More Action Ahead

Cycling offers plenty of options. You can choose to ride a sleek, lightweight road bike to travel long distances. Or you can climb steep mountains on a bike decked out with shocks, gears, and fat tires.

All bikes and riders rely on science to perform at their highest level. Science techniques continue to improve bike designs. These complex machines get lighter, smoother, and faster every day.

## POPULAR ANNUAL BIKE EVENTS

| RACE | TYPE OF CYCLING | WHEN | WHERE |
| --- | --- | --- | --- |
| Tour de France | Road Racing | June-July | France & nearby countries |
| Giro d'Italia | Road Racing | May | Italy & nearby countries |
| BMX World Championship | BMX | Varies | Location changes each year. |
| Leadville 100 | Mountain Bike | August | Colorado Rockies |
| Cyclo-cross Nationals | Cyclo-cross | January | Location changes each year. |
| Summer X Games | BMX Freestyle | Varies | Los Angeles, CA |

What are you waiting for? Hop on a bike and turn your energy into motion!

# GLOSSARY

**acceleration** (ak-sel-uh-RAY-shuhn)—the rate of change of speed

**aerodynamic** (ayr-oh-dy-NA-mik)—built to move easily through the air

**air resistance** (AIR ri-ZISS-tuhnss)—the force the air puts on an object moving through it

**axle** (AK-suhl)—a bar in the center of a wheel around which the wheel turns

**calorie** (KA-luh-ree)—the measure of the amount of energy in food

**carbohydrate** (kar-boh-HYE-drate)—a nutrient that provides energy

**center of gravity** (SEN-tur UHV GRAV-uh-tee)—the point at which an object can balance

**centrifugal force** (sen-TRI-fyuh-guhl FORS)—an outward push an object experiences as it moves in a circular path

**dense** (DENSS)—closely packed together

**double** (DUH-buhl)—two steep hills close together on a BMX race course

**electrolyte** (i-lek-TRAH-lyte)—a mineral, such as sodium, potassium, magnesium, or calcium, which helps produce and store energy and regulate fluid in the body

**force** (FORSS)—a factor (such as pushing or pulling) that causes something to change its speed

**friction** (FRIK-shuhn)—the resistance caused by one surface moving over another

**gravity** (GRAV-uh-tee)—a force that pulls objects towards the center of Earth

**half-pipe** (HAF-pipe)—a U-shaped ramp bikers use to perform jumps and other maneuvers

**kinetic energy** (ki-NET-ik EN-ur-jee)—the energy of movement

**mass** (MASS)—the amount of matter in something; matter is anything that has weight and takes up space

**momentum** (moh-MEN-tuhm)—the force or speed created by movement

**rolling resistance** (ROHL-ing ri-ZISS-tuhnss)—the force resisting the motion of a body rolling across a surface

**slipstream** (SLIP-streem)—a path of moving air behind a moving object

**tension** (TEN-shuhn)—the stress, such as tightness or stiffness, that results from stretching or pulling

**traction** (TRAK-shuhn)—the amount of grip between two surfaces in contact with each other

**turbulent air flow** (TUR-byuh-luhnt AIR FLOH)—air flowing off a moving object with different directions and velocities

**velocity** (vuh-LOSS-uh-tee)—the speed an object travels in a certain direction

# READ MORE

**Bow, James.** *Cycling Science.* New York: Crabtree Pub. Co., 2009.

**Graham, Ian.** *The Science of a Bicycle.* New York: Gareth Stevens Pub., 2009.

**Petrie, Kristin.** *Bicycles.* Everyday Inventions. Minneapolis: ABDO, 2008.

# INTERNET SITES

FactHound offers a safe, fun way to find Internet sites related to this book. All of the sites on FactHound have been researched by our staff.

Here's all you do:

Visit *www.facthound.com*

Enter this code: 9781476539096

# INDEX